Baxter the Retriever

A Giant-Sized Hunting Dog with a Giant-Sized Personality

JOHN TROY

Skyhorse Publishing

Printed in China

For Emily, Anya, Chetan, and Jaden

Foreword

In this book you will meet Baxter, the large, lovable, impulsive, black retriever, who loves hunting. His adventures will give you an inside look into the way he thinks and acts. A dog's point of view, if you will. This sometimes frustrates his owner, but in the long run, Baxter is always loved.

His owner finds hunting from a boat doesn't work out too well—he falls into the water when Baxter jumps in to retrieve the ducks! Or, how about catching a fish and asking Baxter to "throw it in the live well with the others" as it lands in Baxter's mouth? My wife and I did own a similar dog, Rontu, who shows up in some of these cartoons. He would jump into the water, catch those sunnies, and eat them! One day he actually jumped into shallow water headfirst from our canoe and got his head stuck in the mud.

You will see Baxter retrieving a pheasant and surprising his owner by bringing it back with two other dogs attached. "Does this qualify for a double?" wonders the owner.

Picnics are one of Baxter's favorite things! But not when he accidentally eats the jalapeño hot dog sauce! And, watch out! If you sit next to the water while having your picnic, you will definitely find yourself wet when he jumps into the water.

It's a challenge to bring along Baxter's lunch, which is heavy enough to be mistaken for an overnight backpack. Even Santa has a challenge when he sees Baxter's stocking hung by the fireplace.

Then there is the problem of finding a vet who wants to treat Baxter as "all the vets recommend taking Baxter to a large animal vet." That's also a problem when looking for a doghouse. They just don't make them big enough! On the plus side, Baxter's owner never has to take his children to go pony riding.

These are only some of the adventures that will make you laugh and think about the pets you have owned doing some of these very same antics.

What could be more comforting than waking up in the middle of the night and reaching down to feel your dog lying on the floor at your side of the bed. We all know the joy of having pets, and they will always have a place in our hearts. The memories of all these moments will last forever.

—John Troy, 2012

Editor's note: John Troy passed away in December 2012. He will be remembered fondly.

"I've been here a week and no salmon. Baxter jumps in—bingo."

"Who would've thought Baxter would be retrieving us?"

"...and then Paul Bunyan said to Babe, his blue ox..."

"No, Baxter, you're supposed to chase them, not sit on them!"

"How did you know I took Baxter fishing this morning?"

"That fence keeps the deer in, but it sure doesn't keep Baxter out!"

"We must be near a tennis court."

"That was Joe Naylor in Waupaca; Baxter's howling woke him up last night. Say, isn't Waupaca six miles from here?"

"There must be another way to try out my new Super Duper Tuna Bustin' outfit!"

"No, no, Baxter . . . DON'T RETRIEVE . . . STOP . . . it's small game season!"

"I have the whole trail to myself since I started running with Baxter."

"If it wasn't for Baxter grabbing me by the seat of my pants, that catfish would've dragged me in!"

"We *are* sitting in a boat, and a *small, overloaded one* I might add."

"He thought if Snoopy could sit on his dog coop, he could, too."

"Baxter doesn't know his own strength, *but they do.*"

"Actually, I didn't bag them; Baxter stepped on them."

"No, no, not roll over! Sit up, sit up!"

"He sure saves me a lot of towing charges."

"Trouble is, Baxter flushes the whole field."

"Good, we don't have to chop any holes."

"I sure wish Baxter would drink out of his water dish."

"His dog coop's plenty big enough, until he stands up, or wags his tail."

"Hey, *no goal tending!*"

"No! Retrieve is when you put it in your mouth and bring it to me. Don't throw it!"

"Guess who won the tractor pull!"

"We'll take that one."

"What happened at the sporting goods store? Does 'bull in a china shop' ring a bell?"

"Well, it's not like he's really begging."

"Baxter likes to feel at home."

"No, it's not an overnight backpack, it's Baxter's lunch."

"Who ever heard of a citation for a dog blocking a trout stream?!"

"All I know is Baxter jumped in, and here I am!"

"You should have thought of that before we left the doggie run!"

"All the vets recommend taking Baxter to a *large animal* vet."

"I think Baxter is carrying his 'squirrel technique' too far!"

"Baxter won an award at the dog show . . . for not stepping on the other dogs."

"We had a good day duck hunting—Baxter only tipped the boat over three times."

"If you don't mind, I'll do my own retrieving!!"

"Remember the tree that used to be in the front yard that you tied Baxter to this morning?"

"Whoa, it's 'give me your paw' and there goes the old back!"

"If that sixty-pound catfish bites on this line, he's in for a big surprise!"

"We couldn't get him a big enough doggie door, so we just got him a key."

"Baxter won first prize. He was the only dog to retrieve two geese and another dog at the same time!"

"Fish and Game wants us to keep Baxter out of the woods during bear season. He's scaring them all out of the state."

"No, *that* one is Baxter's, *this* one is ours."

"Baxter is having a low self-esteem day."

"A little advice . . . don't stand in front of Baxter when you holler 'fetch.'"

"It's a good thing we're not on a 'catch and release' lake!"

"To Baxter, life is one small meal after another."

"No, Baxter wasn't the pick of the litter, he *was* the litter."

"Baxter should win the Nobel Peace Prize."

"When you play with Baxter, there's no such thing as touch football!"

"Baxter pulled this little guy out of the creek. Now he wants to keep him."

"Fetch, Baxter, fe . . . $@*#!"

"How do I find out if the ice is safe? Baxter, go ahead!"

"Guess which one is Baxter's."

"Now THAT'S an ALL-WEATHER RETRIEVER!"

"Chuck, I don't like the way your dog backs up a point."

"Baxter needs a new dog dish. One he can't eat."

"Ed's horse got sick."

"From now on, let *me* get the mail!"

"Door, Baxter, *door!*"

"First day of trout season has a different meaning to Baxter than it does to most of us."

"Wow, almost got robbed! Final score: Baxter two, muggers nothing!!"

"Wait a minute! My gun! ... my boots! ... my...."

"Now how are we going to drag this moose out . . . say!"

"He's a hunting dog—why can't he do his aerobics outdoors?!"

"We came in first in the six-dog sled team competition."

"Another Bigfoot sighting reported from Waupaca. Didn't you and Baxter go hunting there yesterday?"

"No, it's not the army corp of engineers digging a channel. It's Baxter looking for a downed duck."

"Looks like two other dogs are after Baxter's duck. Whoops, make that three."

"Run for high ground! Baxter is coming!"

"Hard to believe Baxter is a descendant of wolves and Russian tracking dogs."

"Down in front, and stop drooling on Roseanne!"

"Amazing how that bull knows the difference between a fly rod and a shotgun!"

"COULD WE HAVE A LITTLE LESS ENTHUSIASM EVERY TIME I CATCH A FISH?!"

"... and where it says 'eight tiny reindeer,' we'll change it to one BIG reindeer."

"Now that we get soft Frisbees for Baxter, he stopped breaking them—instead he eats them!"

"I don't know what's chasing Baxter, but take my word for it . . . RUN!"

"BAXTER *SIT! GO SIT!*"

"Stop wagging your tail!"

"Alright, alright, get in! I'll take you fishing!"

"With Baxter, it doesn't do rabbits any good to hole up."

"I *know* two is the limit. I have no idea where he got the *other* one."

"Hard to believe we're looking at a dog that can hit a deer fence and clear it by two feet."

"That's the last time *you* start the motor!"

"Oooh, fly fishing can be expensive—Baxter just knocked down a lawyer."

"Do you have to howl every time I miss a fish?!"

"Sorry, Baxter's into instant gratification lately."

"*This* is why I bring Baxter on fishing trips."

"To tell you the truth, I'd rather he *treed* them."

"I think we'll sleep under the stars tonight."

"Is this your largest one?"

"Here they come, Baxter, so don't move—or we'll sink!"

"...and here's Baxter's puppy picture—he's the black one."

"Either you sit in the front of the boat or we don't leave the dock!"

"I know all about the 'leash law,' ma'am. On the way back, I'll explain it to Baxter."

"OKAY, OKAY, SO I MISSED! KNOCK IT OFF ALREADY!"

"Baxter had twelve tennis balls in his mouth . . . now he can't shut it."

"It's one of those mutual respect things."

"You know that big catfish that's been pulling everybody in? Well, wish him luck this time!"

"BAXTER!"

"The boom came around and hit Baxter in the head, so he bit it off!"

"This is one of Baxter's 'build a little dog's ego' days."

"*Who* made these muddy tracks?!"

"To Baxter, *all* game is *small* game."

"Funny, but we don't seem to have any neighborhood bullies."

"You'd be surprised what we save on pony rides."

"Just think of what we save on pack mules."

"...adding in Baxter's food bill puts us right around the poverty level."

"Uh-oh, here comes your retriever, and it looks like it's going to be an interesting day."

"Guess what Baxter retrieved today."

"Baxter! Hunting season is over—STOP RETRIEVING!"

"Baxter is getting into a scrap with the town bully. He doesn't know it yet."

"Baxter gives a whole new meaning to the term 'split rail' fence."

"Uh-oh, Baxter's collar is hung up on the fence line again."

"That's some hunting dog you have there, pal!"

"Now is that a perfect point or is that a perfect point?!"

"There you go, Bax, one sandwich for me, one for you. One loaf enough?"

"Oh, I'd say about twenty-five horsepower."

"The anchor? Just a precaution."

"I hate it when Baxter falls in love!"

"He *is* on a leash. Look!"

"Whoa, low tide, Bax!"

"Okay, okay, who rolled that ball under my chair?!"

"That's our refrigerator, and this big one is Baxter's."

"He's too big for a doggie jacket, and I had this old overcoat, so…"

"Baxter, WAIT!"

"When it comes to snowshoes, you can't beat Baxter!"

"…so I said, 'Why get a horse?'"

"It's a note from the farmer. It says, 'Please repair the gate after Baxter goes through it.'"

"I never knew what a joy hunting was until I hunted with Baxter. Read into that what you will."

"Baxter's depressed. He saw a Clydesdale horse this morning, and it was bigger than him."

"Honey, was that the cat? Sounded like she wanted out."

"No more high-energy, protein-loaded dog biscuits for Baxter."

"Go ahead, Baxter, test the ice for us ... unless you have a better idea."

"Yessir, Baxter loves to retrieve in cold weather."

"I don't care if they are your best friends, STOP GIVING OUR GEESE AWAY!"

"Baxter didn't feel good, so I put him in the laundry room to…"

"I have the feeling it's going to be a rough winter."

"Of course, there's always the possibility it *fell apart*."

"Baxter's my kind of dog alright. Matter of fact, he's my kind of rhino, hippo, elephant . . ."

"Good nose, Baxter, you're going in the right direction."

"So begins a new chapter in Baxter's book: Why Beg If You Can Steal It?"

"You've got ours? Good, I'll grab Baxter's."

"Nice point, Bax, but let me do the flushing."

"You could at least try to *act* like a hunting dog!"

"A coop, Bax, is for warmth and shelter, not to lie on!"

"We should register his tail as a dangerous weapon!"

"FETCH . . . whoops, too loud."

"Don't worry, it's only up to Baxter's ankles."

"No, no, Baxter, retrieve . . . RETRIEVE, NOT SWALLOW!"

"I wonder if they have support groups for between-seasons retrievers?"

"Fetch…WHOOPS!"

"Baxter's not what you would call a 'finesse fisherman.'"

"NEVER *EVER* TELL BAXTER TO *JUMP* IN THE BOAT!"

"Hey, this beer is warm!"

"I'm not sure I want to be remembered that way."

"We got thrown out of the zoo; Baxter was scaring the lions."

"Black bear season is open."

"Guess who found out about electric fences!"

"No, I'm not rowing over to the duck!"

"Hey, I'm watching the ball game!"

"We had that tennis ball custom-made. He kept swallowing the small ones."

"No, no, Baxter, we already got that one!"

"There you go, Bax, *now* let's see who's the *fastest retriever in the state!*"

"I just said 'save me,' Bax, not 'drag me home!'"

"With Baxter around, who needs a bearskin rug?"

"Whoa, pardon me pal! For a silly minute there, I thought that was my duck."

"Does this qualify as a double?"

"Doctor, it's about Baxter's killer instinct…"

"I don't feel like going hunting today."

"Boy, vet prices are up! $160 for a crumpled examining table, $185 for a smashed front door..."

"Why do we even bother walking across on the rocks to stay dry?!"

"...then how about one of these old swinging doors, like in Western movies?"

"Here's the vet bill—$25 for Baxter's shots plus $350 for the office damage."

"Yup, scratches from a bear marking its territory. Looks like a big one, too."

"We're running out of trees."

"Baxter won an award at the dog show for the Dog Least Likely to Be Attacked by a Bear."

"That must be Baxter."

"So you painted Baxter so hunters won't shoot him. Isn't that nice."

"YOU TAKE HIM RIGHT BACK WHERE YOU FOUND HIM!"

"Dogs are *supposed* to be cold and to shiver after retrieving a duck!"

"Here's another one, Bax. Throw it in the livewell with the others."

"Uh-oh, somebody ate our jalapeño hot dog sauce!"